COULD YOU EVER

DINE WITH DINOSAURS!?

Written by
Sandra Markle

Illustrated by
Vanessa Morales

Scholastic Inc.

For Courtney Chamberlin and all the children of North Elementary School in Noblesville, Indiana.

Acknowledgments: The author would like to thank the following for sharing their enthusiasm and expertise: Dr. Reese Barrick (*Giganotosaurus*), Fort Hays State University, Hays, Kansas; Dr. Luis Chiappe (*Shuvuuia*), Natural History Museum of Los Angeles County, Los Angeles, California; Dr. Denver Fowler (*Velociraptor*), Dickinson Museum Center, Dickinson, North Dakota; Dr. Gregory Erickson (*Tyrannosaurus rex*), Florida State University, Tallahassee, Florida; Dr. James Kirkland (*Utahraptor*, Timeline), Utah Geological Survey, Salt Lake City, Utah; Dr. Matthew Lamanna (*Carnotaurus*), Carnegie Museum of Natural History, Pittsburgh, Pennsylvania; Dr. Hans Larsson (*Ambopteryx*), McGill University, Montreal, Quebec, Canada; Dr. Stephan Lautenschlager (*Allosaurus*), University of Birmingham, Birmingham, United Kingdom; Dr. W. Scott Persons (*Tyrannosaurus rex*, *Microraptor*), College of Charleston, Charleston, South Carolina; Dr. Paul Sereno (*Spinosaurus*, *Suchomimus*), The University of Chicago, Chicago, Illinois

A special thank-you to Skip Jeffery for his loving support during the creative process.

Photos ©: 1: sakala/Alamy Stock Photo; 4, back cover: Shutterstock.com; 6: Daniel Eskridge/Stocktrek Images/Getty Images; 8: Gabriel Ugueto; 10: Elena Duvernay/Stocktrek Images/Getty Images; 12, back cover: Sergey Krasovskiy/Stocktrek Images/Getty Images; 14: Warpaintcobra/Getty Images; 16, back cover: Shutterstock.com; 18: Dennis Wilson/Pangaea Designs; 20: MasPix/Alamy Stock Photo; 22: MR1805/Getty Images; 24: Sergey Krasovskiy/Getty Images; 28 left: Shutterstock.com; 28 right: Shutterstock.com.

Text copyright © 2024 by Sandra Markle
Illustrations copyright © 2024 by Vanessa Morales

Library of Congress Cataloging-in-Publication Data available

ISBN 978-1-338-85871-6

10 9 8 7 6 5 4 3 2 1   24 25 26 27 28

Printed in the U.S.A.   40
First edition, March 2024

Book design by Maria Lilja

What if one day when you woke up, you weren't quite yourself? What if your whole world had changed? What if you were in the long-ago past dining with dinosaurs? *CARNIVOROUS** DINOSAURS!*

Carnivorous (kar-NI-vuh-ruhs) means meat eater.

Tyrannosaurus rex (tie-RAN-oh-SAWR-us rex)

Tyrannosaurus rex was a BIG carnivore. The largest weighed over 16,000 pounds. It was a little over 42 feet long and 13 feet tall at the hip. *T. rex* walked leaning over to watch for prey. And it attacked teeth first! Its mouth was full of around 60 big, strong teeth with sharp, jagged edges like a steak knife. Plus, powerful jaw muscles gave *T. rex*'s bite bone-crunching force.

When you dine with *Tyrannosaurus rex*, be sure you are on the guest list, not the menu.

FACT

Scientists are not sure how fast *T. rex* could move. But some think it ran as fast as 25 miles per hour to catch prey.

Velociraptor (veh-LOSS-ih-RAP-tor)

Velociraptor was only the size of a turkey, but it was fast. And it could shift left or right while running flat out. It did that with quick swings of its rod-stiff tail. That let it catch up to smaller dinosaurs, lizards, and rat-sized animals. Then, lifting its tail straight up, it stopped and pounced.

When you dine with *Velociraptor,* you will eat fast food—if you can catch it!

FACT

Velociraptor used the big, hooklike claw on the second toe of each foot to stomp and stab prey.

Ambopteryx (am-bop-TAIR-icks)

Ambopteryx was the size of a squirrel. With long, claw-tipped fingers and toes, it climbed trees and scrambled along branches. Spreading its bat-like wings, it glided from tree to tree to escape predators and dine on insects.

When you dine with *Ambopteryx*, your grub will be bugs. YUM!?

FACT

Ambopteryx had buck teeth. Its longer, forward-tilted front teeth made its bite just right for snagging flying insects.

Spinosaurus (SPY-nuh-SAWR-us)

Spinosaurus was a GIANT carnivorous dinosaur. It weighed 20,000 pounds and was 45 feet long. Its crocodile-like head was 6 feet long. Imagine what a BIG mouth full of sharp teeth it had! It easily caught fish for breakfast, lunch, and dinner.

When you dine with *Spinosaurus*, you can bet what you are served will be FIN-tastic!

FACT

Spinosaurus's broad back feet had long, flattened toe claws to help keep it from sinking while walking in muddy places.

Utahraptor (YOU-tah-RAP-tor)

Utahraptor weighed 800 pounds, was 17 feet long, and 6 feet tall. This biggest of all raptors was a master ambush attacker. It hid until prey came close. Then it leaped. And, while holding on tight, it repeatedly kicked prey with its 12-inch-long, sickle-shaped toe claws. *Utahraptor* was a Super Stabber Raptor!

UTAHRAPTOR STEAK HOUSE
·100% TOE TENDERIZED·

When you dine with *Utahraptor*, you will enjoy the most tender steak ever!

FACT

Utahraptor's 5-inch-long front claws were curved like giant eagle talons.

Giganotosaurus (jee-gah-note-uh-SAWR-us)

Giganotosaurus weighed 17,000 pounds, was 43 feet long, and 12 feet tall at the hip. It usually had its big head lowered, ready to bite. And its giant jaws were armed with 76 BIG, knifelike teeth. Since it could run 30 miles per hour, any prey *Giganotosaurus* chased was likely its next meal.

DINO Soufflé

CHEESY MAC
AND DINO

DINO EGGS
BENEDICT

DINO PIZZA

BARBECUE
DINO RIBS

When you dine
with *Giganotosaurus*,
it will be an
all-you-can-eat
beast feast.

FACT

Giganotosaurus, like most
carnivorous dinosaurs, had
new teeth growing under
each tooth. So, old teeth
were pushed out, keeping its
bite sharp.

Carnotaurus (kahr-no-TAWR-us)

Carnotaurus weighed 4,000 pounds, was 26 feet long, and 9 feet tall. Its arms were so tiny they were possibly useless. However, it had the biggest horns of any carnivorous dinosaur. Though only 6 inches long, these were perfect for head-to-head combat when two males battled for a mate. Or when one Carnotaurus wanted to dine alone.

When you dine with *Carnotaurus*, WATCH OUT! Your host is not good at sharing.

FACT

Carnotaurus had a thick, muscled neck it used to swing and deliver powerful head blows or strong shoves.

Shuvuuia (shoo-VOO-yah)

Shuvuuia was a skinny little dinosaur the size of a chicken. Its BIG eyes let it successfully hunt at night. And it ran fast on long legs to chase down rat-sized animals, lizards, and insects. Once close, Shuvuuia snapped up prey with its mouthful of tiny, sharp-edged, peg-like teeth.

When you dine with *Shuvuuia*, you will share a moonlit picnic. Be glad it's too dark to clearly see what you are eating!

FACT

Shuvuuia had short, strong arms with a GIANT claw at the tip.

Allosaurus (a-luh-SAWR-us)

Allosaurus weighed 4,400 pounds, was 16 feet long, and 10 feet tall. While it looked like a shorter, skinnier *T. rex*, there was one big difference. *Allosaurus*'s jaws were extra flexible. So, to attack prey, it opened its mouth SUPER wide. Then its strong neck slammed its upper jaw, lined with 3-inch-long, knifelike teeth, into prey. WHAM! DINNERTIME!

Allosaurus

Welcome **BIG BITE CONTEST** TODAY!

01:10:00

BIG Bite

When you dine with *Allosaurus*, do NOT agree to a **Big Bite Eating Contest**.

FACT

Allosaurus had longer arms than *T. rex*. And, instead of just two claw-tipped toes, it had three to grab and hold prey.

Suchomimus (SOOK-oh-MY-mus)

Suchomimus weighed 10,000 pounds and was 35 feet long. It was 12 feet tall at the hip and plodded along with its 4-foot-long snout pointed down, ready to snap. With 122 backward-curving teeth, it caught its fill of small prey on land and in shallow water.

When you dine with *Suchomimus*, you will eat fish so fresh your dinner may try to escape.

FACT

Suchomimus's large, curved thumb claws were perfect fishhooks!

Microraptor (MIKE-row-rap-tor)

Microraptor was the size of a crow. Both its arms and legs were feathered, but it lacked strong muscles to flap and fly. So, it used its claw-tipped fingers and toes to climb high and swoop down. It had a mouthful of bladelike teeth with the front teeth tilted slightly forward. These were perfect for spearing, then biting fish, birds, and ratlike animals.

When you dine with *Microraptor*, you will grab a snack on the go.

FACT

Microraptor, like all raptors, had a raised, inside toe with a BIG claw.

So, if you could dine with *CARNIVOROUS DINOSAURS*, which dinosaur host would you choose?

Luckily, you don't have to decide. You will always live when you do and dine with people, too.

WHAT MADE A DINOSAUR A DINOSAUR?

Dinosaurs were a group of reptiles that roamed Earth for millions of years, long ago. By comparing the bony skeletons of dinosaurs to modern reptiles, such as crocodiles and lizards, scientists discovered key ways dinosaurs were different. Today, most reptiles have a hip structure that makes their legs sprawl out on either side of their bodies. So, they can only lift their bellies a little way off the ground. They must swing their bodies side to side to walk forward. But a dinosaur's skeleton put its legs directly below its hips for better body support. That let a dinosaur lift its belly off the ground. Dinosaurs could stand, walk, and run on just their two hind legs.

T. rex

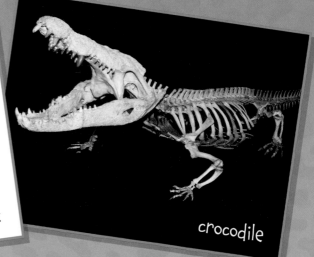

crocodile

WHAT MADE CARNIVOROUS DINOSAURS SUCCESSFUL?

Carnivorous dinosaurs were the meat-eating dinosaurs that had to catch prey to eat. To be a successful carnivore, a dinosaur needed excellent eyesight, keen hearing, and, if possible, a good sense of smell to find prey. It also helped if the dinosaur was camouflaged to blend in until it was close enough to ambush prey.

Once prey was discovered, a carnivorous dinosaur needed to catch it to be successful. Strong legs and the ability to jump, run fast, or swoop down helped. Jaws with lots of sharp teeth were important. Claws for grabbing or stomping and stabbing were also useful. And it helped a carnivorous dinosaur be successful if it was not a picky eater. Then it ate whatever it could catch.

WHEN DID DINOSAURS LIVE?

Not all dinosaurs lived at the same time. Check the timeline to see when each of the featured dinosaurs was alive.

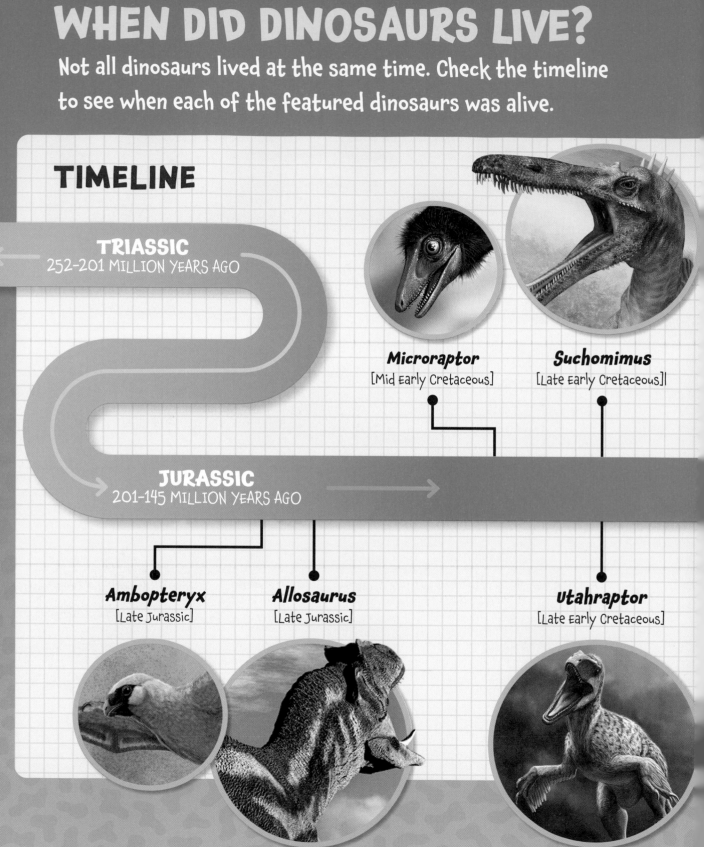

TIMELINE

TRIASSIC
252–201 MILLION YEARS AGO

Microraptor
[Mid Early Cretaceous]

Suchomimus
[Late Early Cretaceous]|

JURASSIC
201–145 MILLION YEARS AGO

Ambopteryx
[Late Jurassic]

Allosaurus
[Late Jurassic]

Utahraptor
[Late Early Cretaceous]

Giganotosaurus
[Early Late Cretaceous]

Velociraptor
[Late Late Cretaceous]

Tyrannosaurus rex
[Latest Late Cretaceous]

CRETACEOUS
145–66 MILLION YEARS AGO

Spinosaurus
[Early Late Cretaceous]

Carnotaurus
[Early Late Cretaceous]

Shuvuuia
[Late Late Cretaceous]

Timeline data
provided by
Dr. James Kirkland

FUN FACTS!

Carnotaurus's tiny arms had ball-and-socket shoulder joints, so its arms could probably wave. Scientists believe such moves might have been to attract a possible mate's attention.

Tyrannosaurus rex's two powerful legs and feet with claw-tipped toes were good weapons to kick and stomp prey or any competing *T. rex*.

Velociraptor had feathers on its front legs, and flapping them helped it stay steady on its feet as it shifted directions while running fast.

Utahraptor had unusually thick leg bones. That made its legs strong enough for superpowered kicks.

Allosaurus had a very flexible tail that kept it balanced during speedy prey chases.

Velociraptor